YEARS
of the
NATIONAL
BUILDINGS
RECORD
1941-1991

with an introduction by
Sir John Summerson

ROYAL
COMMISSION
ON THE HISTORICAL
MONUMENTS
OF ENGLAND

Introduction © Sir John Summerson 1991
Text and pictures, unless otherwise attributed,
© Royal Commission on the Historical Monuments of England 1991

First published 1991 by Trigon Press, Beckenham, in conjunction
with the Royal Commission on the Historical Monuments of England
to accompany the exhibition: '50 Years of the National Buildings
Record'

British Library Cataloguing in Publication Data
50 years of National Buildings Record.
  1. Great Britain. Architecture. History 2. Great Britain
  720.941

  ISBN 0-904929-27-2
  ISBN 0-904929-28-0 pbk

Designed by Andrew Shoolbred
Co-ordinator Judith Sheppard
Printed in Great Britain by BAS Printers Limited,
Over Wallop, Hampshire

Front cover: Corn Exchange, Leeds, West Yorkshire. G.B. Wood 1941
Back cover: Winderton, Brailes, Warwickshire. Christopher Dalton 1973

ACKNOWLEDGEMENTS

The Royal Commission is grateful for permission to reproduce photographs in the National Buildings Record of which the copyright is held by Paul Barkshire, B. T. Batsford Ltd, Country Life, the Courtauld Institute of Art, Millicent Godfrey, the Howarth-Loomes Collection, Oxfordshire County Council, Richard Palmer, Sir John Summerson, and the Warburg Institute. The captions to the illustrations give details of the photographer, when known, the date taken and the provenance or copyright when it is other than our own.

In addition to those members of staff named in the Secretary's foreword, the following have provided invaluable assistance: Janet Atterbury, Robert Blow, John Bold, Priscilla Boniface, Henry Bosanquet, Terry Buchanan, Nicholas Cooper, Moira Hegarty, Jean Irving, Kathryn Morrison, Jacqui Ramsay, Phillis Rogers, Tony Rumsey, Joanna Smith, and Dorothy Stroud. At Trigon Press Judith Sheppard and Roger Sheppard have taken a personal as well as a professional interest in this publication, which has been designed by Andrew Shoolbred. To all those named and any inadvertently missed the Royal Commission is indebted.

This book celebrates a half century of achievement by the National Buildings Record (NBR). Founded in the darkest days of the Second World War, the NBR has become the principal national repository for records of historic buildings, and since 1963 it has been part of RCHME's National Monuments Record. The NBR today continues to stand as a monument to the foresight and perseverance of its creators, and we are extremely fortunate that Sir John Summerson, its prime mover and first Deputy-Director, has contributed an introduction to this publication. The Royal Commission is indebted to him and to the others who have assisted, most importantly Mr Cecil Farthing who joined the embryo NBR in 1941 and retired as Curator in 1976.

This publication complements and builds upon the anniversary exhibition held at the Victoria and Albert Museum in April 1991. This is an appropriate venue, for it was at the V & A that the NBR held its first post-war exhibition in 1945 to demonstrate the great achievement of those first few difficult years.

A generous contribution towards the cost of the exhibition has been made by The Landmark Trust, and the Royal Commission is pleased to acknowledge this assistance and the interest shown by the Trust's former chairman, Sir John Smith.

I am grateful to all those present members of staff who have prepared this volume and especially to Stephen Croad, Head of the NBR, who conceived and co-ordinated this exhibition and publication. The text and captions have been written by Sarah Brown, Anna Eavis, Diana Hale, Ian Leith and Anne Woodward. The photographs were printed by Tom Patterson, Marcela Pfeiffer and Alma Samuels of the Royal Commission's photographic staff. Many others, too numerous to mention individually, have assisted in a multitude of ways and further details are given in the acccompanying acknowledgements. However, special thanks should be given to Kirsty Cook, whose design for the exhibition has had a considerable influence on the over-all appearance of this book.

The photographs published here are but a sample of the wealth of illustration held for the public in the NBR. In its fiftieth year, the archive contains some $1\frac{1}{2}$ million photographs dating from the earliest years of photography in the 1840s to the present day.

As Secretary to the Royal Commission on the Historical Monuments of England it gives me great pleasure and pride to acknowledge the great debt we owe those who have created the National Buildings Record we know today and to be sure that it will go from strength to strength in the future.

Tom Hassall
Secretary
Royal Commission on the Historical Monuments of England
Fortress House
23 Savile Row
London W1X 2JQ

INTRODUCTION

The National Buildings Record (NBR) was founded in 1940 under conditions of peculiar stress and urgency. Between the declaration of war in September 1939 and the first serious air assaults on London in September 1940, much energy had been directed towards the protection of the nation's artistic heritage. Works of art, archives and antiquities of every movable kind had been evacuated from urban centres and distributed in remote country houses or the slate quarries of Wales. Immovable objects of moderate size and special importance were protected by sandbags built around steel frames. What defied all measures of protection were *buildings*. They had to take their chance, to be remembered by posterity, if the worst should happen, either as ruins, ambiguous rebuildings or through such illustrations, graphic and photographic, as had been accidentally assembled and preserved or published over the years.

In 1939 there was no institution exclusively concerned with the recording of architecture. The nearest was the Royal Commission on Historical Monuments, but its obligations extended only as far as Queen Anne and its main function was to make inventories of pre-1714 structures; its plans and photographs, though of the highest quality, were more or less incidental. The terms of the Royal Commission might have been enlarged *ad hoc* for a special wartime function but nobody, apparently, had thought of this and its investigators and photographers had already been dispersed. A small residuary staff was established in Cambridge, at Pembroke College, guarding its archives.

Where London was concerned there was that industrious and dedicated body, the London Survey Committee, founded in 1894 by C.R. Ashbee precisely for the purpose of making and publishing records of doomed or endangered buildings in the London area. This was a voluntary body, and had neither the means nor the personnel to cope with the cosmic emergency which the war had brought about. There were other voluntary bodies interested but, in the circumstances, impotent.

In these discouraging circumstances, what could be done? In the first year of a world war whose duration and intensity no-one could foresee, the instant creation of a national archive of architecture was pure fantasy. It did seem to some, however, that measures might at least be taken to draw and photograph damaged buildings before they were totally demolished, to list buildings in towns and cities likely to be subject to air raids, and provide for such photography or measured surveys as might be judged urgently necessary.

In 1939, various interested parties outside the Civil Service addressed themselves to the problem. As I recall the circumstances, the most effective promoter in the first instance was the Librarian of the Royal Institute of British Architects, the late E.J. ('Bobby') Carter. Carter had been appointed in 1931. He had reorganised the RIBA Library in its new quarters in Portland Place and had acquired a reputation as one of the most energetic and enthusiastic officers of the Institute, always ready to promote cultural or humanitarian initiatives within the architectural field. He had done much for the employment of refugee architects from Hitler's Germany. Now the salvation and amplification of architectural records was brought to his notice and immediately attracted his interest. It was natural for anybody concerned with such questions to look to the RIBA and its Librarian for advice and I was among those who did so, for reasons to which I will come presently. I found Carter fully conscious of the situation and already in touch with various individuals and societies who had expressed anxiety. He asked me to prepare a paper for discussion and at the same time wrote to Sir Kenneth Clark, the Director of the National Gallery, who was conspicuous at the time for what he was doing to encourage the preservation of cultural values from negligence on the one hand or panic shut-down on the other.

Clark's response was to suggest that the RIBA should hold a conference of societies and individuals likely to be interested. The conference took place at the RIBA on 18 November 1940 and with W.H. Ansell, its president, in the chair. Thirty-three delegates represented eighteen societies, with myself as one of two representing the Georgian Group. There seems to be no record of the proceedings but the RIBA *Journal* printed (16 December 1940) a memorandum drafted by Carter which had been taken as a basis of discussion and which reflects my earlier conversations with him. The conference agreed unanimously that what was needed in the circumstances was a recording agency under the control of a National Advisory Council. A committee was appointed, consisting of W.H. Ansell (President, RIBA), Sir Kenneth Clark, Walter H. Godfrey and J.E.M. Macgregor (of the Society for the Protection of Ancient Buildings), to work out a plan in detail and to approach the Minister of Works and Buildings, with a view to obtaining his co-operation.

This committee met on 25 November, one week after the conference. Carter had prepared an agenda accompanied by a draft plan such as the conference had suggested. It was on a fairly grand scale. The running costs were estimated at over £10,000 per annum. The committee quickly scaled this down, reducing the scheme to a directorate of two – one to look after the centralisation of information and records, the other to be in charge of war-damage activities – with appropriate secretarial assistance. Sir Kenneth Clark approached Lord Reith, the newly appointed Minister of Works and Buildings.

By 30 December the membership of the Advisory Council had been settled. Sir Wilfred (later Lord) Greene, Master of the Rolls, had accepted the office

Sir John Summerson
As an architectural journalist working in London, John Summerson recognised the threat to historic buildings from wartime bombing and helped initiate the events which resulted in the formation of the NBR. He became Walter Godfrey's deputy and travelled all over the country compiling lists of buildings at risk. In 1947 he left to become Curator of Sir John Soane's Museum, but has maintained close links with the NBR throughout its 50 years.

FRANK OTLEY c1940, © Sir John Summerson

Walter Hindes Godfrey (1881-1961)
An architect and antiquary with a passion for recording historic buildings, WHG (as he was usually known) was an excellent choice to become Director of the NBR at its foundation. After the war he was responsible for the restoration of the Temple Church and Chelsea Old Church following bomb damage. He retired as Director of the NBR in 1960.

ELIZABETH FRANK c1940, © Mrs Millicent Godfrey

of chairman. There was a membership of ten: W.H. Ansell, G.H. Chettle (Ministry of Works and Buildings), A.W. Clapham (President, Society of Antiquaries), Sir Kenneth Clarke (Director, National Gallery), the Earl of Crawford and Balcarres, Mrs Arundell Esdaile (the authority on church monuments), H.S. Goodhart-Rendel (Past President, RIBA), the Dean of Norwich (Chairman, Central Council for the Care of Churches), Sir Charles Peers and Professor A.E. (later Sir Albert) Richardson. The Council first met on 6 January 1941, and at this meeting Godfrey was named as Director and myself as Deputy Director. It was now a question of finance.

The Council first appealed to the Government for support and the Treasury, through Lord Reith's instrumentality, made a grant to enable the framework of the organization to be set up at once. This made it possible for the two appointments to be confirmed. Additional funds were to be solicited from individuals and charitable trusts. They came eventually from the Leverhulme, Rockefeller and Pilgrim Trusts.

The choice of Walter Godfrey (1881-1961) as Director was an excellent one. He was a man of 60, an architect, an antiquary of integrity and long experience and with a passion for recording architectural antiquities. As a young man he had edited and mostly written the four Chelsea volumes of *The Survey of London* and was still closely associated with the committee's work, which he continued to edit throughout the war. He had also initiated the Architectural Graphic Records Committee in 1931. As a personality he was amiable and soft-spoken but there was also a strain of stubborn egotism which made him a difficult man with whom to exchange ideas. As Director of the NBR he set himself to realise the ambition of a lifetime – the creation of a national archive of architecture – and to do so without compromise and in his own way. Wartime restrictions and the stupidity and indifference of people who did not come up to his expectations made him a chronic grumbler, but in the circumstances his quiet obstinacy had a good deal to recommend it.

My own participation in the formation of the Record came about in the following way. In 1940 I was employed as assistant editor of *The Architect and Building News*, a weekly professional journal. Architectural journalism was in the doldrums, with little to write about except the latest hare-brained devices to protect people and property against bombs. It happened that in the previous year, I had prepared a course of lectures on 18th-century London architecture for the Courtauld Institute of Art. These were cancelled owing to the turn of events but a publisher had persuaded me to expand these lectures into a short book. In consequence I spent much time walking the streets of London and photographing Georgian buildings, especially of the kind that had never been photographed or even noticed. This was in that pacific period of twelve months which was called the 'phoney war'. The bombs began to fall in September 1940. My photographic ramblings continued but now with an increasing sense of urgency, not to say alarm, and the idea of the book was given up. It seemed now a good deal more important to record buildings than write about them. One amateur photographer, however, with a Leica camera, could hardly make much impression, quite apart from the fact that photography of bomb-damaged buildings was strictly forbidden to anybody not armed with an official permit. Buildings of considerable interest were being wrecked every night and the remains often cleared as rubble without further thought. This was sad and I foresaw the same thing happening on a horrifying scale, and not only in London. Could not, should not something be done? I sought Carter's opinion, as I have said, and was thus drawn into the early stages of the affair. In due course I was invited to assist Walter Godfrey as his deputy.

It was on 3 February 1941 that Godfrey and I sat down together in a room at the RIBA with blank sheets of paper in front of us, and considered how to begin to execute the functions with which we had been entrusted. What soon emerged was that we had rather different views about priorities. Godfrey's main concern was with the co-ordination of existing records. I was more anxious to set photographers to work without delay on buildings in London and other vulnerable areas – especially buildings of which existing records were certainly either negligible or non-existent. As it turned out, this divergence of interests made it possible for us to work in harmonious inter-dependence, Godfrey undertaking the administration and co-ordination, I the executive recording.

The RIBA provided temporary accommodation – a committee room on the first floor at 66 Portland Place. Secretarial help was needed and Godfrey recruited his own secretary, Miss Griffiths, a good-natured and highly competent lady with an undeviating loyalty to 'WHG' (as Godfrey was mostly referred to). A second secretarial post was filled by Dorothy Stroud, who had been working for Christopher Hussey at *Country Life* and had acquired there a valuable working knowledge of architectural history. Hearing of the NBR proposals on the BBC, she had promptly written to Sir Kenneth Clark to ask about a possible vacancy. Clark passed her letter to Godfrey and Godfrey passed it to me. Dorothy was interviewed and engaged. We were now a working team, but a very small one indeed, charged with initiating a programme of architectural recording which would have taxed an organization ten times the size. Fortunately, perhaps, we did not see it quite like that at the time.

Two things needed to be done as soon as possible. The first was to identify the areas liable to be raided and to list the buildings within them most obviously needing record. The other was to find photographers capable of doing the work, and willing to do it. This was not easy. Our budget was restricted. Even the 10s 6d flat rate charged by professionals working for the architectural journals mounted to excessive totals when extensive coverage of a building was required. We needed photographers in various parts of the country or willing to travel. In London, Herbert Felton, with whom I had worked for some years on the *Architect and Building News*, was the first to come to an arrangement which fitted the case. He was a ruddy, grey-haired bohemian with a generous heart, a schoolboy sense of humour; a fine photographer but with an incorrigible preference for picturesque views over disciplined recording. He worked mostly in London but came with me on

Cecil Farthing
Seen here working in the NBR's wartime offices at All Souls College, Oxford, with one of the small band of assistants and the familiar red box files. As Conway Librarian at the Courtauld Institute of Art, Cecil Farthing transferred with the Conway's photographs and remained with the NBR when the collections were divided again at the end of the war. He became Walter Godfrey's deputy in 1947 and succeeded him as Director in 1960. Cecil Farthing retired in 1976.

c1942, © Mrs Millicent Godfrey

occasional excursions to bombed or threatened cities and produced vast quantities of negatives, some a good deal better than others. S.W. Newbery, a more conventional character, was another recruit from my journalistic days, whom we employed from time to time. In Bristol we found R.J. Wills, an excellent architectural photographer, much of whose coverage of Bath was eventually published in Walter Ison's classic description of that city. In the West Country, Margaret Tomlinson, architect and skilled amateur photographer covered, among other things, the Exeter ruins before they disappeared. In Leeds, a strict Baptist conscientious objector, G. Bernard Wood, plodded usefully along with lists of mostly coal-black Gothic churches and classical warehouses in coal-black cities. But the greatest discovery and the champion producer of results of the highest competence was G. Bernard Mason. He was an experienced craftsman with a small business in Birmingham which folded, or was about to do so, early in the war. Photography was a sideline but when it was suggested to him (I think by an acquaintance of Godfrey's) that he might like to be associated with our work he took up the challenge with dedicated seriousness, delivering great parcels of negatives, all of high competence, punctiliously numbered and listed. He lived in Birmingham where, among other activities, he and his wife kept bees and made mead which he bottled for their friends. My difficulty was to keep him supplied with adequately detailed programmes of work. Nothing was too much trouble for him, even to unfixing and replacing a radiator which obstructed the view of a monument in some obscure church in a much bombed coastal town. He produced thousands of negatives in many different parts of the country and the NBR owes a great deal to his drive, patience and skill. His outstanding contribution was recognised after the war by the award of an MBE.

Much of my time was spent in compiling information and in doing the research necessary to the making of sensible lists, and in securing facilities for our photographers to have access to interiors. Looking back, it is curious to reflect how little at that time anybody knew or cared about English urban architecture of the 19th century. The Victorian architecture of the City of London, of Leeds, Manchester, Bolton, Bradford and Bristol was unmapped. I had to go to contemporary sources, spending long evenings of Firewatch duty searching the *Builder* and the *Building News*, fortunately still available on the shelves of the RIBA Library. Through 1941-2 I spent much time moving round England in the tracks of the raiders. From August 1941, the following cities and towns crop up in my diary, some more than once: Leeds, Hull, Newcastle, Dover, Ramsgate, Liverpool, Derby, Canterbury, Colchester, Cambridge, Norwich, Yarmouth, Exeter, Worcester, Gloucester, Bath, Bristol, King's Lynn, Reading, York, Salisbury, Portsmouth, Rochester, Ely, Winchester, Chester, Rye, Winchelsea, Chippenham, Coventry, Cheltenham, Bury St Edmunds, Lowestoft and Manchester.

In September 1941 the NBR established itself at Oxford, where All Souls College provided office space, shelf room for the records and a bedroom for Godfrey. I remained in London, at the RIBA with Dorothy Stroud who, besides secretarial work, undertook listing in the outer suburbs, her very thorough lists being followed up partly by Felton and partly by Mason.

Meanwhile, Godfrey had made an important move towards the co-ordination of existing records. The Courtauld Institute was naturally interested in what we were doing, especially because it possessed what was

Fredrick Palmer (d 1990) *left* and **Herbert Felton** (d 1968)
Two of the NBR's photographers planning a wartime sortie – note the hoods on the Morris's headlamps showing that blackout regulations were still in force. Herbert 'Leo' Felton was the NBR's first professional photographer, appointed in May 1941. After the war he continued to record buildings throughout England and Wales, while Fred Palmer concentrated on East Anglia and south-east England.

R.A. PALMER 1945, © *Richard Palmer*

probably at the time the largest existing photographic collection of English architecture and sculpture in the country – about 100,000 negatives. Anthony Blunt, Deputy Director of the Courtauld, discussed the possibility of collaboration with Walter Godfrey, with the result that the architectural section of the Courtauld collection was made available to the NBR. The collection had been evacuated to Hatherop Castle in Gloucestershire but was now, in the autumn of 1941, moved to Oxford. At the same time, Cecil Farthing, the Courtauld Institute's photographic curator, agreed to join the Record at Oxford. The shelving for the boxes of prints came with the photographs and was, not without difficulty, installed in the rooms at All Souls. The negatives were deposited for security in the basement of the Bodleian Library where space was lent for the duration of the war by Bodley's Librarian, Dr (later Sir Edmund) Craster.

The accession of the Courtauld collection formed a valuable nucleus for the Record. There was, however, one immediate difficulty: it was arranged for teaching purposes, according to periods and types. It fell to Farthing to rearrange the whole in topographical order by counties, a task which he accomplished single-handed in a month. It was only then that it became possible to recruit secretarial staff to feed the new material into the Courtauld boxes, as it came to hand, titling and indexing the negatives in the process.

As the NBR became better known, it attracted material from benefactors of many kinds: amateur photographers, owners of collections of negatives

Amesbury Road, Moseley, Birmingham, West Midlands

On two consecutive nights in July 1942 Birmingham was heavily bombed, apparently in retaliation for a British raid on Hamburg. This photograph, taken on 29 July, illustrates damage sustained on the last night of the raid. Though it is not of great architectural importance, this house is nevertheless a good example of a typical suburban home. The photographer, James Nelson, was the NBR's representative for Warwickshire, living in nearby Cotton Lane, Moseley.

JAMES NELSON 1942

Nos 27-32 Southernhay West, Exeter, Devon
Only the façade remained of this late
Georgian terrace in the centre of Exeter after
the air raids of 1942. Mrs Tomlinson,
architect and skilled amateur photographer,
was the NBR's representative in the west of
England, recording Exeter throughout the
blitz. This area outside the medieval city wall
was built by Matthew Nosworthy between
1790 and 1810. These ruins were demolished
later in 1942, but similar elegant terraces
which had sustained only minor war damage
were often the victims of drastic clearance
policies.

MARGARET TOMLINSON 1942

and people possessing measured drawings. Godfrey incorporated the indexes
of the Graphic Records Committee in the NBR and formed a liaison with
the Central Council for the Care of Churches. As the flow of material increased,
so did the secretarial staff, composed mainly of Oxford ladies of talent and
goodwill, content to earn a rather moderate wage. By the end of the war
there was a secretarial staff of 15.

The NBR acquired useful allies. A.W. Clapham, a member of our Council
and Secretary of the Royal Commission on Historical Monuments in its
hideout at Pembroke College, Cambridge, undertook, with those of his col-
leagues who had not been called up or seconded to various wartime depart-
ments, to cover parts of East Anglia. Quite independently of the NBR, the
Warburg Institute had, at a very early stage, obtained facilities to photograph
monuments in Westminster Abbey and St Paul's Cathedral and produced
beautiful work. Amateur photographers in many parts of the country came
to us with offers of voluntary help. There was, in short, plenty of goodwill.
Rarely were we denied facilities to carry out our investigation and photography, even the Naval Dockyards at Portsmouth and Devonport relaxing their
security so that their 18th-century shipbuilding yards and officers' residences
could be photographed.

In September 1942 we were able to report to the Council that of 172 towns
selected where buildings had been identified as deserving of urgent record,
67 had been taken care of and 21 were in hand: the work proceeded through
1943 when there was a lull in raiding and the sense of urgency relaxed. In
1944, however, the flying bomb or 'doodle-bug' made its unwelcome entry,
the Dulwich Art Gallery and the hall of Staple Inn being among its early victims. A still more sinister weapon, the V2 or long-range rocket, Hitler's last

desperate device to bring England to its knees, then started its offensive. It was during the period of doodle-bugs and rockets that the Council decided to hold the first exhibition of the NBR's work and other associated activities, in a room at the National Gallery made available by Sir Kenneth Clark. There was a press day on 1 June 1944, the exhibition opening on the following day when I broadcast a piece about it for the BBC. At the time, news of D-day was hourly expected and an exhibition of photographs and drawings of historic buildings was somehow not an event to stir the public's imagination very deeply. There was a good attendance, however, and it passed off without discredit.

It is easy now, half a century later, to see the wartime years of the NBR as pathetically inadequate to the needs of the time. As a collection of material intended to forestall widespread destruction it arrived decades too late. The devastation of most of the City churches occurred before the NBR had got on its feet. (I think I am right in saying that Hawksmoor's church, St George in the East, was the only London church of consequence whose interior was recorded before it was gutted by fire in 1940.) A list of significant buildings destroyed in the blitz without adequate record would be formidable. In the long run, however, the NBR's wartime achievement was far from negligible. The records of bombed cities in their ruinous state are a part of architectural and topographical history now completely blotted out by rebuilding, and it could be said that more destruction of historic buildings took place after 1945 than during the years of the blitz. By 1944, the date of the first Town and Country Planning Act to make provision for the protection of historic buildings, the NBR was in being as a national archive of architectural records. As such it has developed alongside the statutory measures which followed one another in the 1950s and 1960s. Walter Godfrey's vision of a national archive of architecture has amply justified itself. It is one of the ironies of history that it took a national emergency of colossal dimensions to bring it to birth.

JOHN SUMMERSON

The 1940s

The immediate needs after the foundation of the NBR in 1941 were to acquire extensive records of buildings as quickly as possible. In this endeavour the creators of the archive were eminently successful. The most important acquisitions included the Conway Library of photographs belonging to the Courtauld Institute of Art and such historic collections as the negatives of the Victorian photographer, Henry Taunt of Oxford.

The dedication of the small band of pioneers is illustrated in this letter written by Walter Godfrey from his quarters at All Souls College, Oxford, to which the NBR had been evacuated in 1941:

> ... 8.45 when I walk across to the Common Room for breakfast. We lunch in a delightful little Buttery, built by Hawksmoor, the architect, in the shape of an egg, oval in plan and vaulted ... I work till 6.30 and then we dine in the Common Room at 7.00 and I get back after our talk and coffee to a bit more work before bedtime.

In response to the desperate wartime situation and in an attempt to preserve surviving historic buildings, the government passed the Town and Country Planning Act in 1944. This empowered the embryo Ministry of Town and Country Planning to prepare lists of buildings of special architectural or historical interest worthy of preservation, based upon those begun by the NBR's staff and its nationwide network of contributors. The 1944 Act was complemented by the 1947 Town and Country Planning Act which empowered local authorities to preserve historic buildings whether or not the owners wanted them preserved. These new arrangements and powers were to have long-term effects on the work of the NBR.

Vicars' Close, Wells, Somerset

The Vicars of Wells served in the Cathedral in the place of absent prebendaries. In 1348 Bishop Ralph of Shrewsbury formed them into a College and provided them with houses. The Vicars' Close is a fascinating survival of a mid 14th-century planned street, 456 ft long. The front gardens were added by Bishop Bubwith c1410-20 and although the houses have been altered internally, their external appearance remains largely unchanged. Brian Clayton's large photographic output concentrated on medieval subjects and was passed to the NBR soon after its formation along with other negatives amassed by the publishing firm of B.T. Batsford.

B. CLAYTON 1920s, © B.T. Batsford Ltd

Blockley, Gloucestershire

Henry Taunt (1842-1922) of Oxford covered most of the villages of his own county as well as all the surrounding ones for his commercial photographic business. Most of the surviving whole-plate glass negatives are held by the NBR and they provide an unrivalled regional archive. They were acquired in the early 1940s from Oxford Library.

H.W. TAUNT c1890, © Oxfordshire County Council

Mount Edgcumbe, Maker with Rame, Cornwall

Mount Edgcumbe was yet another casualty of wartime bombing raids. On 22 April 1941 incendiary bombs gutted the house and destroyed its contents. On the recommendations of the War Damage Committee a programme of rebuilding began in 1958 under the supervision of the architect Adrian Gilbert Scott. In spite of wartime damage the main lines and fabric of the original 16th-century structure have been preserved, and the grounds are now a country park.

c1900, Gerald Cobb Collection

Coventry, West Midlands

All too often, it was only after bomb damage that the NBR's photographer could record what remained, but even these photographs impart valuable information. Sometimes, as here, the view formed a panoramic sequence from a high vantage point. From Trinity Church the medieval street pattern is evident despite the disappearance of the timber buildings consumed by the fire which left only steel-framed buildings standing.

JAMES NELSON 1941

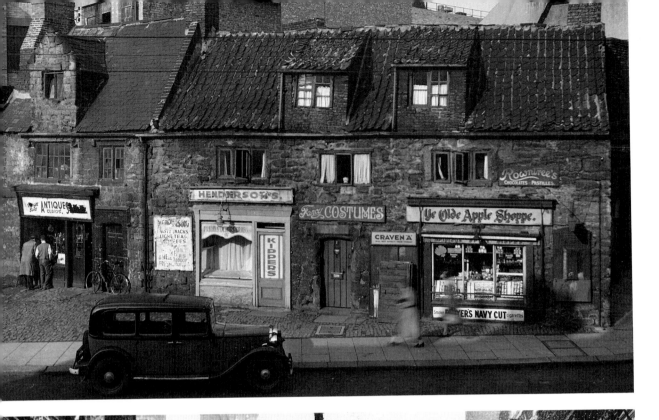

Percy Street, Newcastle upon Tyne, Tyne and Wear

By the 17th century, when these stone cottages were built, Newcastle was already an impressive town. Writing in 1697, Celia Fiennes was impressed by the many buildings 'lofty and large of brick mostly or stone'. The wartime recording effort today defines not just the built fabric but also the social conditions: the advertisements and shop fronts tell us as much about the society of 1943 as they do about the cottages.

G.B. WOOD 1943

Holland House, Kensington, London

The grand Jacobean country house became in the early 19th century one of the most celebrated meeting places for artists, writers and celebrities in London. On the night of 27 September 1940 incendiary bombs dropped on the west wing of Holland House caused a fire which destroyed all but the east wing of this remarkable house. This photograph taken soon after the fire gives an almost surreal impression as the library browsers seem oblivious of the devastation around them. Holland park and the house had been opened to the public after the First World War, but it was not until 1952 that the London County Council purchased the estate. The surviving part of the building is now a youth hostel.

FOX PHOTOS 1940

West Street, Lewes, East Sussex

The historic county town of Lewes was described by Defoe as 'a fine and pleasant town, well built and situated'. However, on 20 January 1943 at 12.42 pm, peace was shattered when six high explosive bombs fell on North Street and the surrounding area. This photograph taken immediately after the raid shows an all too familiar wartime scene, with police, air raid wardens, first-aid workers and civilians tending the injured and attempting to create order out of chaos.

20 January 1943, *Sussex Express*

Oriel House, Nos 30 - 32 Farringdon Street, City of London

The fire brigade turntable ladder is probably involved in making safe the ruins of No 30 Farringdon Street after the raid of 29 - 30 December 1940. Oriel House was built in 1884 and was the office of Babcock and Wilcox Ltd, engineers. This dramatic roof-top view is one of a number of photographs of the Fleet Street area taken by the designer of the *Daily Express* crusader logo while firewatching at the newspaper's offices.

E.L. MATTO 1940

East Cowes Castle, Cowes, Isle of Wight
John Nash designed Cowes Castle for himself
as a rural retreat where he could live as a
country gentleman. He lived there from 1798
until his death in 1825. During the Second
World War it was requisitioned by the
Government for use by British troops. Sadly,
during that time it was badly damaged and
was eventually demolished. The photograph
was taken just before demolition in 1949.

G.B. MASON 1949

**New Bridge Street Goods Station, Newcastle
upon Tyne, Tyne and Wear**
The mass and classical decorative veneer of
this North Eastern Railway goods depot are
more reminiscent of the Chicago style than of
contemporary English industrial architecture.
The building was destroyed in an air raid in
1941. The local photographic firm of Harry
O. Thompson supplied the NBR with early
views of Newcastle and the North-East during
its formative years.

H.O. THOMPSON 1920s

Church of St Martin le Grand, Coney Street, York

For over an hour on the night of Tuesday 28 April 1942, York suffered what the indignant British press termed a 'spite' attack. It was the German press that first coined the phrase 'Baedeker Raid' for those retaliatory attacks launched against England's historic cities, referring to Karl Baedeker's famous guidebooks. York lost its medieval guildhall and the nearby parish church of St Martin. This photograph, taken by Alderman Morrell while the debris still smouldered, shows the clock (installed in 1856) stopped at 3.45 am. From 1961-6 a partial repair of the church was undertaken, preserving the tower, the south aisle and part of the west end. The area of the chancel and north aisle now contains a memorial garden.

J.B. MORRELL 29 April 1942, *Northern Echo*

Great Charlotte Street, Liverpool, Merseyside

Between August 1940 and August 1942 Liverpool experienced 90 air attacks, the most serious being the infamous 'May week' beginning on the night of Thursday 1 May 1941, which was to claim the lives of 1,900 people. On the night of Saturday 3 May, when Lewis's department store (to the right) and much of the area around Lime Street Station was destroyed, 218 aircraft bombed the city. This photograph, received by the NBR in March 1942, shows the people of Liverpool going about their business without a second glance at the devastation around them.

J.E. MARSH & SONS 1941

Canterbury, Kent

This photograph shows the aftermath of a Baedeker attack in May 1942. Canterbury, which in Hitler's opinion was 'a main centre of English hypocrisy', was bombed in direct retaliation for an RAF raid on Cologne that killed approximately 470 people. This view shows the resulting damage to St Augustine's Abbey and neighbouring buildings

1942 *Central Office of Information*

Church of St Benedict, Norwich, Norfolk

The 11th-century parish church of St Benedict was photographed by Ernest Rahbula, the RCHME's senior investigator, in July 1941. The Royal Commission's small residuary staff removed to Cambridge in June 1940 had undertaken a rapid survey of historic buildings and sites thought to be at risk. The value of this record can be appreciated from the second photograph; Norwich was the target of Baedeker raids on the nights of 27 and 29 April 1942. St Benedict's was one of the casualties and its ruins were recorded for the NBR in May. Only the tower, now designated a Grade 1 listed building, survives today.

Above ERNEST RAHBULA, RCHME 29 July 1941

Above right G.B. MASON May 1942

Dean Fotherby Monument, Canterbury Cathedral, Kent

The apparently clear distinction between documentary and 'art' photography might be called into question by the surveys of Cathedral monuments carried out by Bill Brandt for the NBR in 1941: some of his images evince an eye not normally found in the work of those who merely document. The tomb to Dean Fotherby (d 1619) has its sides arrayed with skulls and bones, a common representation of mortality.

BILL BRANDT 1941

Market Place, Dunster, Somerset
The octagonal Yarn Market of c1589 with its
dormers and pyramidal roof which sweeps
down almost to the ground provides a
contrast to the otherwise linear street plan of
the little town. Dunster's picturesque street
dominated by the castle has proved a constant
lure for artists – note the painter with his easel
in this view. The photograph was one of
those included with the collections of the
Courtauld Institute which formed the nucleus
of the NBR's holdings in 1941.

F.T.S. HOUGHTON C1910

**The Ring, Blackfriars Road, Southwark,
London**
Built in 1782 as the Surrey Chapel for the
Revd Rowland Hill, a non-conformist
preacher who attracted large and enthusiastic
congregations. In 1881 it closed and
subsequently became a famous boxing arena,
known as The Ring. This photograph, taken
after bomb damage in 1940, reveals the
octagonal inner rotunda designed by William
Thomas. The building was subsequently
demolished.

SPORT AND GENERAL 1940

Corn Exchange, Leeds, West Yorkshire

The Leeds Corn Exchange was designed by the Hull-born architect Cuthbert Brodrick and built between 1861 and 1863 by two Leeds firms at a cost of £15,000. Its elliptical plan may derive from the irregularity of the site, but Brodrick was probably influenced by the (much earlier) circular *Halle au Blé* in Paris. The detailing of the doorways and plinth is reminiscent of 16th-century Roman models. The building housed 56 offices and is covered by an iron-framed dome which reaches a height of 75 feet above floor level.

G.B. WOOD 1941

Upper Arcade, Bristol, Avon

Bristol's Upper and Lower Arcades were built in the mid 1820s by James Forster as part of
the street improvement scheme. Designed in the classical style with pitched glass roofs, it is
said that they were inspired by Samuel Ware's Burlington Arcade in London's Piccadilly. The
medieval centre of Bristol suffered very badly during the war and large areas of the city
remained waste ground for some years after. The Lower Arcade survived the bombing but the
Upper Arcade was less fortunate as this 1941 photograph illustrates.

VICTOR TURL 1941

The
1950s

As the NBR approached the end of its first decade of existence, a new danger presented itself. Its *Annual Report* for 1949-50 stated:

> Today the incidence of heavy taxation and the scarcity of building materials have brought harassed owners of country houses and house-breaking firms together, with the result that buildings are being dismantled that can no longer be maintained, and fine architecture is being reduced to the stone, brick and timber from which it was once superbly fashioned.

The Town and Country Planning Acts had failed to stem the tide of destruction. The NBR's photographers were diverted from routine recording to cope with the new demand, and their coverages of houses dating from the Middle Ages to the 19th century remain an enduring record of much fine architecture that has been lost. Working alongside investigators from the Royal Commission, which from 1956 allocated staff to record historic buildings under threat, the same photographers extended their range to include traditional architecture throughout the country.

Collections acquired during this period extended the detailed coverage of the fittings of ancient churches and cathedrals, especially monumental sculpture. The negatives by Sydney Pitcher of medieval architecture and vernacular buildings, and Helmut Gernsheim's photographs of the important tombs in St Paul's Cathedral and Westminster Abbey taken for the Warburg Institute during the war, are among other important acquisitions of the 1950s.

As the archive grew, so the extent of the task of providing a survey of ecclesiastical, domestic and civic buildings of every type, as well as architectural detail, sculpture, woodwork, glass and fittings, became apparent.

Heath Old Hall, Warmfield cum Heath, West Yorkshire

The village of Heath was once described as a 'village of mansions' for there are two imposing Georgian houses and formerly there was an important Elizabethan house, Heath Old Hall. Built for John Kay in 1584-95, it is one of a small and distinctive group of houses which was clearly influenced by the architect Robert Smythson. After use by the military in the Second World War, it fell into disrepair and was demolished in 1961.

HERBERT FELTON 1954

Hadlow Castle, Hadlow, Kent

Closely modelled on, albeit more sturdily constructed than, Beckford's Fonthill, the octagonal tower at Hadlow is now almost all that remains of Walter Bouton May's eccentric Gothick castle of c1838-40. The tower, of brick and Roman cement, was built by the engineer and naval architect George Ledwell Taylor. The principal architect of the house was the little-known J. Dugdale, although May's Gothick mausoleum in the nearby churchyard suggests the patron's very personal involvement.

J. MECKLENBURG 1951

Rievaulx Abbey, North Yorkshire

Ryedale provided the sort of remote site well loved of the Cistercian order, which arrived here in 1131. In the mid 12th century the Abbey housed 140 monks and 600 lay brethren. The present church, dating from the 13th century, is second only to Fountains for the extent of its Cistercian remains.

HERBERT FELTON 1953

Left

Chapter House, Wells Cathedral, Somerset
The polygonal Chapter House is one of the
most distinctive features of the English Gothic
cathedral. The late 13th-century octagonal
example at Wells is one of the most
impressive of all. While the vault of
Westminster Abbey's Chapter House rests on
a column with 16 ribs, the Wells vault rests
on 36. This striking view was part of Herbert
Felton's NBR coverage of cathedrals.

HERBERT FELTON 1952

St Paul's Cathedral, City of London
Helmut Gernsheim (b 1913) came to England
from Germany in 1937. His talent as an
architectural photographer is amply
demonstrated in this and the many other
photographs he took of St Paul's Cathedral
and Westminster Abbey on behalf of the
Warburg Institute. His fame rests largely on
his influential work *The History of Photography*
(1955); his record of these two London
monuments, photographed when they were
under real threat of destruction, continues to
be one of the most consulted parts of the NBR
collections.

HELMUT GERNSHEIM 1942, © *Warburg Institute*

**Music Room, Sun Street, Lancaster,
Lancashire**
Tucked away and until recently hemmed in
by later buildings is the extraordinary and
unexpected Music Room of c1730-40,
described by Pevsner as 'the finest interior in
the town'. Built on three storeys, the principal
room is on the first floor and contains
elaborate stucco decoration in the Italian style.
In 1957, when this record photograph was
taken, the future of the badly decayed
building, then embedded in a toy warehouse,
was extremely uncertain; indeed, Pevsner
despaired of it. Its future was assured by its
acquisition by the Landmark Trust.

G.B. MASON 1957

The 1950s

Church of St Peter and St Paul, Charing, Kent

To the west of the impressive late 15th-century tower lies the gatehouse range of a former palace of the Archbishops of Canterbury. Although the Domesday record suggests the existence of pre-Conquest archiepiscopal buildings, the present remains indicate a building period encompassing the late 13th to 16th centuries. The gatehouse was probably built in the first half of the 14th century by Archbishop John Stratford who was particularly fond of Charing. Henry VII was entertained here in 1507 and in 1520 Henry VIII lodged here on his way to the Field of the Cloth of Gold.

F.J. PALMER 1953

Holy Trinity Church, Long Melford, Suffolk

Photographed by Herbert Felton as part of the NBR post-war coverage of Suffolk, this view of Long Melford church displays its Perpendicular-style elegance to excellent effect. The apparently harmonious appearance of the chancel, nave and tower belies its more recent architectural history. The imposing west tower was only constructed in 1898-1903, replacing an 18th-century brick tower recorded in a photograph of 1894, also held by the NBR.

HERBERT FELTON 1955

Chinese Dairy, Woburn Abbey, Bedfordshire
In the late 18th century the purpose of a dairy
for a country house estate had as much to do
with fashion as utility. This photograph
shows the covered entrance-way to the dairy
built in 1794 to the designs of Henry Holland
with decorations added by John Crace and
John Theodore Perrache. Black marble,
Japanese and Chinese dishes, painted flowers,
figures and birds all contribute towards a
flamboyant and visual display.

G.B. MASON 1949

**Home Farm Barn, Dowdeswell,
Gloucestershire**
This photograph, taken before the Second
World War, shows a late 16th to mid 17th-
century barn in use for its traditional purpose,
the processing of a grain crop. Although
protected by inclusion in the Statutory Lists,
part of the Home Farm complex, of which the
barn is the most impressive building, has now
been converted into a house, the fate of many
disused farm buildings, destroying
irrevocably the integrity of the farmstead.

SYDNEY PITCHER c1920

The 1950s

Left

Bowood, Calne Without, Wiltshire

This photograph taken around 1910 shows the house and the parterre and is a superb illustration of the formal classical garden design at Bowood. The upper terrace was created by Smirke in 1817-18. Barry added the link building in 1835-6. The house was demolished in 1955, but the stable block (left) remains, converted into a new house. The photographic firm of Newton & Co specialised in photographing country houses and their surviving negatives were acquired in 1951.

NEWTON & CO C1910

Kersey, Suffolk

Kersey is probably one of Suffolk's most picturesque villages. This image shows the mixture of styles and materials which are representative of Suffolk's vernacular architecture, although exposed timber framing is untypical of the county. This photograph was taken by Fred Palmer who was one of the mainstays of NBR photography in the 1950s. It is also representative of the rural bias of the county photographic surveys taken in the 1950s.

F.J. PALMER 1959

Right

Coleshill House, Coleshill, Oxfordshire

This important house, one of only five major houses designed by Roger Pratt, was built from the later 1650s to 1662. It contained one of the most beautiful mid 17th-century staircases in England but in 1952 after a major fire at the end of a restoration programme the whole house was pulled down – the fate of many other country houses.

1919, © Country Life

Queen Victoria's Bedroom, Stoneleigh Abbey, Warwickshire

Shortly before the disastrous fire which closed this large and complex house for 24 years, the interiors were recorded, thus considerably facilitating the detailed restoration work by showing the state of the furnishings and decoration. Hallam Ashley was another of the NBR's band of stalwart photographers, contributing to the collections from the 1940s until the 1980s.

HALLAM ASHLEY 1959

Roof Boss, Angel Choir Aisle, Lincoln Cathedral, Lincolnshire
Constructed c1256-80 to house the shrine of St Hugh, the Angel choir is named for the famous angels that adorn its main elevation. In its aisle vaults it also boasts some of the finest mid 13th-century roof bosses, this one depicting intertwined dragons. C.J.P. Cave specialised in the study and photography of English medieval roof bosses, constructing an enormous lens to make this possible without the aid of scaffolding. His collection was acquired by the NBR in the early 1950s.

C.J.P. CAVE 1929

Church of St Nonna, Altarnun, Cornwall
This early 16th-century bench end is one of 79 made by one 'Robert Daye' who signed the figure of St Michael. In the Middle Ages the church claimed to possess the relics of the Welsh saint St Nonna, although she died in Brittany and was buried in a fine tomb at Dirinon (Finistère).

HERBERT FELTON 1957

Westminster Abbey, London
The gilt-copper effigy of Edward III was completed after his death in 1377 and lies on a marble base in the Confessor's Chapel at Westminster Abbey. Although the head is based on a wooden portrait made at Edward's death the drapery is stiff and stylised. The king is portrayed as if vested for coronation, with lavishly decorated robes and slippers. The cushion on which his feet once rested has gone. The tomb was probably designed by Henry Yevele who was later commissioned by Richard II to produce a similar monument for himself and his Queen, Anne of Bohemia.

HELMUT GERNSHEIM 1943, © *Warburg Institute*

Alton Towers, Farley, Staffordshire

A.W.N. Pugin, who assisted the 16th Earl of Shrewsbury during the final stages of building at Alton Towers, worked on the chapel from 1837 to 1840, when he wrote that he had been 'fixing figures on the chapel gallery'. The 'figures', now obscured by a false ceiling, take the form of painted and gilt plaster angels kneeling on floriated corbels.

F.J. PALMER 1950

Westminster Abbey, London

Henry VII's tomb, which stands in his chantry chapel at Westminster Abbey, was completed in 1518 and is considered to be the first major Renaissance work in England. The gilt-bronze effigy lies on a base of black and white marble enriched with Florentine putti, angels and floral wreaths. The whole is the work of Pietro Torrigiano whose chequered career included temporary exile from Florence for breaking Michelangelo's nose and a period of service in the papal army under Caesar Borgia. After completing his commission in England he went on to Seville where he was imprisoned by the Inquisition and starved to death in captivity in 1522.

HELMUT GERNSHEIM 1943, © *Warburg Institute*

The Crypt, Worcester Cathedral, Worcestershire
Worcester Cathedral was rebuilt by St Wulfstan after the Norman Conquest. Work began in
1084 and the crypt, which was the site of a synod in 1092, survives from this period. Designed
to house relics, it has ambulatory aisles to allow the free circulation of pilgrims.

HERBERT FELTON 1955

The
1960s

In 1963 responsibility for the work of the NBR and its collections was transferred to the Royal Commission on the Historical Monuments of England. Since the war the two organisations had co-operated closely, particularly over the recording of threatened buildings and in the sharing of photographic services. The Royal Commission's new Warrant empowered it:

> to make such arrangements for the continuation and furtherance of the work of the National Buildings Record ... and for the creation of any wider record or collection containing or including architectural, archaeological and historical information concerning important sites and buildings throughout England.

The amalgamation of the two collections greatly strengthened the NBR by including the systematic surveys which had been carried out by the Royal Commission since 1908.

Threats to historic buildings continued: two of the most famous losses in the 1960s being the Euston Arch and the City of London Coal Exchange. These demolitions highlighted the vulnerability of Victorian architecture which hitherto had been little regarded with few buildings afforded statutory protection.

Interest in old photographs and their value to the historian began to increase in the 1960s and the NBR was able to purchase one of its most important collections: the surviving negatives and a large number of prints by the architectural photographer Harry Bedford Lemere (1864-1944). These high-quality views of houses, public buildings and interior decoration in the late 19th and early 20th century provide an inexhaustible mine of information and telling illustrations.

Left

County Arcade, Briggate, Leeds, West Yorkshire

Frank Matcham, better known as a theatre architect, designed the County Arcade which was built between 1898 and 1900. The interior is richly decorated in terracotta, marble and mosaic. Note the barrel-vaulted roof with its ornate cast-iron arches and balconies. The arches are interrupted by three domes with mosaic pendentives that depict the Arts and Sciences. The arcade has recently been restored to its original splendour.

R.J. WILLS 1961

Round House, Chalk Farm Road, Camden, London

Built in 1847 for the London and North Western Railway as the main locomotive depot serving Euston Station. The Round House was designed by R.B. Dockray. Despite the vast space provided within its 160-foot diameter, it soon proved inadequate for new, larger engines and for over 100 years became a gin warehouse. In the 1960s it achieved unexpected celebrity as an arts centre, the home of Arnold Wesker's *Centre 42*.

R.F. BRAYBROOK, RCHME 1964

Right

The Coal Exchange, Lower Thames Street, City of London

The demolition in November 1960 of J.B. Bunning's Coal Exchange of 1846-9 destroyed what Henry-Russell Hitchcock described as 'the prime city monument of the early Victorian period'. The cast-iron rotunda, surrounded by offices leading off galleries, was decorated with cable motifs recalling mine cables, and encaustic tiles by Frederick Sang depicting collieries, miners and fossilised vegetation.

1958, © *Country Life*

Cammell Laird and Company, Birkenhead, Merseyside

This view of a vast shipbuilding yard taken just before the First World War serves as a useful reminder that not all of Bedford Lemere's large-format negatives are to be associated with genteel domestic scenes. Indeed, like many professional architectural photographers, a substantial portion of his work relates to commercial commissions which are now appreciated as invaluable historical records.

H. BEDFORD LEMERE 1913

The 1960s

The Castle, Corfe Castle, Dorset
The ruins and earthworks of Corfe Castle stand on a natural mound immediately north of the village and are now in the care of the National Trust. This photograph was one of several reproduced in the Royal Commission's *Inventory of Dorset* as part of its systematic survey of the historical monuments of the county. The Royal Commission has employed professional photographers since 1927 to illustrate its many publications and to make comprehensive records.

RCHME 1949

Pembridge, Hereford and Worcester
Herefordshire, because of its isolated rural location and its rich building stock, allows close scrutiny of the local style of timber framing. The 17th-century New Inn with its outbuildings faces the open early 16th-century Market House whose carved posts originally supported an upper storey. The amalgamation of the Royal Commission's photographs after 1963 with those of the NBR greatly enhanced the collection, especially of vernacular buildings.

RCHME 1932

Goosemire, Mardale, Shap Rural, Cumbria
This farmstead was part of a hamlet scattered around Mardale parish church and the Dun Bull Inn. The village was demolished soon after it was recorded for the Royal Commission's Westmorland *Inventory* (1936). The site was flooded in the 1930s with the construction of the dam forming the Haweswater Reservoir. The very top of Wood Hawe in the middle distance is now just above the waters.

RCHME 1935

Warley Village, Halifax, West Yorkshire

The Yorkshire antiquary and author, G.B. Wood, supplied the NBR with many photographs in the 1950s and 1960s. His sympathetic inclusion of the landscape as well as the buildings is brought out here in his depiction of farmland very close to the town of Halifax. The recording of the man-made landscape as well as individual buildings has assumed greater importance in recent years.

G.B. WOOD 1962

Cragside, Cartington, Northumberland

Lord Armstrong's remote retreat was built in 1870 to designs by Norman Shaw. His vigour in handling such a complex scheme is brought out by Bedford Lemere who spent much of his time on extended country house commissions from owners and agents throughout England. His photographs of contemporary and decorative schemes are an endless source of striking illustration and an important record of Victorian and Edwardian taste.

H. BEDFORD LEMERE 1891

Haymount, Holcombe Brook, Bury, Greater Manchester

Bedford Lemere was one of the most renowned architectural photographers of the 19th century. Following his father into the family firm, he died, aged 80, in the office where he started work at 17. The NBR holds most of his surviving negatives, day to day entry books and albums of prints. These are invaluable as a comprehensive survey of late 19th-century domestic architecture and decoration. This print shows a typical Victorian interior with its clutter of furniture, ornaments and potted plants.

H. BEDFORD LEMERE June 1890

Beaupré Hall, Outwell, Norfolk

Beaupré Hall is an example of an early 16th-century manor house. It was built in brick with a central gatehouse featuring polygonal turrets. The manor house passed by marriage from the Beaupré to the Bell family in 1567. Sir Robert Bell, Chief Baron of the Exchequer, added the north-east wing c1570. Beaupré then descended through the Greaves to the Townleys who sold it about 1900. The property fell into disrepair before being demolished in 1966. This striking photograph (right), taken three years before demolition, not only shows its dilapidation but also documents the erosion of the estate for a new housing development. Nothing exists of Beaupré today and houses cover the site.

Above B. CLAYTON 1920s, © B.T. *Batsford Ltd*

Above right F.J. PALMER 1963

Nelson Street, Macclesfield, Cheshire

Although it has medieval origins, Macclesfield grew and prospered as a mill town; the first silk mill was built in 1743 and in the 19th century a large number of cotton mills appeared. During the period after the Second World War a tide of redevelopment changed forever the character of many industrial centres, sweeping away the factories and back-to-back houses. In 1966 Macclesfield was the subject of one of the first Royal Commission photographic surveys of industrial towns. The courts at the rear of these mid-Victorian terraces served as communal washing areas dominated by the outhouse toilets.

R.F. BRAYBROOK, RCHME 1966

Canynges' House, Redcliffe Street, Bristol, Avon

Said to have been the home of the prominent Bristol merchant family who were great benefactors of St Mary Redcliffe church, Canynges' House was demolished in 1937. This 14th-century hall was fortunately recorded photographically by one of many conscientious local antiquarians. This role of recording buildings threatened with demolition or drastic alteration is now carried out nationally by the Royal Commission.

P.E.W. STREET 1933

Halfway Street Farm, Bexley, London

Philip Street, grandson of the High Victorian architect George Edmund Street, methodically recorded in great detail the buildings, such as this farm with oast houses, of his own and the surrounding villages. The photographer's notes, which include details of the buildings' history and painstakingly define the location and vantage point, are invaluable to the NBR.

P.E.W. STREET 1932

Rolleston Hall, Rolleston, Staffordshire
The house of the Mosley family was built in 1871, sold after the First World War and demolished in 1926. This photograph is one of an extensive series taken in 1892 showing the newly redecorated interiors. Each room was decorated in a different exotic style to designs by S.J. Waring and Sons (predecessors of Waring and Gillow).

H. BEDFORD LEMERE 1892

Looseden Barton, Winkleigh, Devon

In Devon a quite distinct local building tradition developed using cob (earth walling) construction, which in order to be kept dry was covered by several layers of rendering. In this 17th-century house the state of the thatch and the rendering suggests that damp penetration has undermined the cohesion of the main building material. It was demolished soon after being recorded.

R.J. WILLS 1963

Rushbrooke Hall, Rushbrooke, Suffolk

Rushbrooke Hall, built on a U-shaped plan, dates from c1550. It was built for Edmund Jermyn but the elevations and interior were partly remodelled in the early 18th century. The interior photograph of the hall illustrates its impressive Georgian stucco decoration. The NBR's photographic survey made in 1955 shows the sad state of repair the building had fallen into before being destroyed by fire in 1961.

HERBERT FELTON 1955

Furness Abbey, Barrow-in-Furness, Cumbria
The London Midland and Scottish Railway Company's large collection of essentially publicity photographs was acquired by the NBR in the 1960s. In this view the arch frames a figure with the Furness Abbey Hotel, built by Paley and Austin between 1846 and 1866, in the background. This hotel was built around the old manor house and next to the railway station. Both were demolished in 1953 and the hotel site was recently excavated by English Heritage.

1892 *London Midland and Scottish Railway Company*

The 1970s

1975 was declared International Architectural Heritage Year and to coincide with this the Royal Commission published a study of English vernacular architecture based on twenty years of recording buildings under threat. These detailed records, including photographs of timber, brick and stone construction, different types of roof, varieties of windows and doors, and traditional decoration, form an important part of the NBR's reference collection.

During the 1970s the study of industrial buildings of all periods increased and what has come to be known as industrial archaeology became a recognised discipline. The NBR had always included specialised buildings and engineering structures, but the archive was greatly enhanced at this time by the acquisition of the collection of railway photographs gathered by the Revd Denys Rokeby and the negatives of wind and water-mills taken by H.E.S. Simmons. Both collections were bequeathed by their compilers, who recognised the importance of depositing the product of their life's work in a national archive where it would be available to future generations of researchers.

The sale in 1977 of Mentmore, the Buckinghamshire country house belonging to the Earl of Rosebery, and the dispersal of its historic contents underlined the need to record buildings, not necessarily threatened with demolition, while still in use with their furnishings and decoration intact. The NBR extended its programme of photographic surveys of buildings of all types – not only country houses, but also such hitherto little regarded types as factories, where the processes and machinery are fundamental to an understanding of the structure.

Holloway Prison, Islington, London
Built in 1848 by J.B. Bunning, the prison began life as the City House of Correction, a place of short-term detention for both men and women. From 1902 it housed women only. In 1970 the 'noble building of the castellated Gothic style' was demolished to make way for a new prison, although the foundation stone inscribed 'May God preserve the City of London and make this place a terror to evil doers' was preserved.

R.F. BRAYBROOK and A.M. RUMSEY, RCHME 1970

Moorswater Viaduct, Liskeard, Cornwall
Cornwall was one of the last regions to be connected with the main railway network, partly because of the considerable number of bridges and viaducts required to cope with the landscape. In order to reduce cost Brunel developed ingenious timber techniques, often in conjunction with local slate or granite piers. In the 1880s the timber stage was replaced by iron girders and today no wooden examples remain in existence.

1860s *Howarth-Loomes Collection*

The Old Hall, Mavesyn Ridware, Staffordshire

The first floor of the 14th-century Gatehouse is open to the crown-post and queen-strut roof which is supported by massive tie beams. On the left the original wall framing with curved braces has been bricked up. The analysis of such construction has allowed much more accurate dating and an understanding of the evolution of regional and national variations.

R.F. BRAYBROOK, RCHME 1971

Canon's Marsh Gasworks, Bristol, Avon

The first Bristol gas company, the Bristol Gas Light Company, began trading in 1816, with a small gasometer called *Aladdin* on a site by the Floating Dock. Demand for gas prompted considerable expansion on the Canon's Marsh site which was the headquarters of the Bristol Gas Company until 1936. The complex was finally dismantled in the early 1970s.

R.F. BRAYBROOK, RCHME 1972

Ring Mill and Mavis Mill, Coppull, Lancashire

Shortly before the First World War Lancashire's vast cotton spinning industry reached its peak, with approximately 85% of its cloth being exported. An impression of the size of these buildings can be gained by comparing the number of spindles each contained. In 1874-5 Oldham had an average of 50,000 spindles per mill, which was twice the national average. Ring Mill and Mavis Mill, built in 1906, contained as many as 100,000 spindles each, indicative of the enormous expansion in mill size by the early 20th century.

JOHN BASSHAM, RCHME 1966

Stonor House, Pishill with Stonor, Oxfordshire

The architectural history of Stonor House is inextricably linked with the fortunes of the Stonor family and English Roman Catholicism. The Stonors have lived here since the 12th century and have celebrated mass in the chapel without a break since the Middle Ages. Parts of the chapel date from the late 13th century.

CHRISTOPHER DALTON 1975

Transporter Bridge, Middlesbrough, Cleveland

The Middlesbrough transporter bridge is one of only four built in Britain. This design allowed the least possible disruption to shipping where a high-level bridge was impractical. A movable platform was slung by cables from a steel framework and carried passengers and vehicles from one side to the other. The bridge shown here was built in 1911 and could accommodate 10 vehicles and up to 600 passengers. This photograph was taken by Eric de Maré who is one of the most important industrial photographers of his generation.

ERIC DE MARE 1955

Swing Aqueduct, Barton, Lancashire

The construction of the Manchester Ship Canal in 1894 heralded a revival in the economic activity of the city and ended a period of depression in local trade. It transformed Manchester into an inland port despite being 55 miles from the sea. The Barton Aqueduct, designed by Sir E. Leader Williams, was the first swing aqueduct to be constructed and was built on the widest section of the canal. It replaced the Bradley Canal aqueduct which was the first fixed aqueduct in England. Hydraulic power was used to swing the aqueduct on its central pier to allow the passage of a ship.

ERIC DE MARE 1955

Baptist Chapel, Ogden, Milnrow, Greater Manchester

The formal extension of the Royal Commission's brief in 1955 to include the recording of buildings threatened with demolition highlighted the need to survey some potentially vulnerable categories. A study of Non-conformist chapels and meeting houses has now been underway for some years. The isolated rural example of chapel and school shown here is typical of the architectural restraint to be found in this type of building.

R.F. BRAYBROOK, RCHME 1970

West Pier, Brighton, East Sussex

The West Pier at Brighton is probably Eugenius Birch's finest pier and possibly one of the most influential in its design. It was in the forefront of iron pier development and set the standards for others to follow. Begun in 1863 and opened to the public on 6 October 1866, it continued the Oriental theme that was expressed in the Brighton Pavilion. Various alterations have been made to the structure, including the provision of greater space for promenading by enlarging the seaward and landward ends. In 1893 a pavilion was added, followed by a concert hall in 1916 and a new top deck entrance in 1932. The pier was finally closed to the public on 30 September 1975 because of severe structural damage : its future is undecided.

TREVOR JONES, RCHME 1970

Elvet Bridge, Durham, County Durham

A bridge has connected the city with the parish of Elvet since c1170. The present ten arches date from the 14th century. In the Middle Ages the bridge had a chapel at each end : St Andrew's to the east and St James's to the west. This undated Campbell's Press Studio photograph, acquired in the early 1970s, depicts the River Wear about 1930.

CAMPBELL'S PRESS STUDIO c1930

Mentmore, Buckinghamshire

This Grade 1 listed house, built 1852-4 by Sir Joseph Paxton and G.H. Stokes for millionaire financier Baron Meyer Amschel de Rothschild, was remarkable for its date in having hot-water heating and artificial ventilation. Decorated and furnished on a palatial scale, the public outcry that accompanied its sale and the dispersal of its contents in 1977 prompted the creation of the National Heritage Memorial Fund.

DENNIS EVANS, RCHME 1976

Church of All Saints, Boyne Hill, Maidenhead, Berkshire

This harmonious combination of church, school and parsonage, constructed of brick with striped decoration of stone and vitrified blue brick, was designed by George Edmund Street, and constructed 1854-7. The contemporary *Ecclesiologist* magazine praised it highly: 'We have seldom been more pleased with a design than the one before us'.

GORDON BARNES 1972

Church of St Peter and St Paul, Winderton, Brailes, Warwickshire
Superbly sited with a view of unspoilt countryside, this church was built 1876-8 by William Smith as a chapel of ease of nearby Brailes. Victim of declining congregations, the church was made redundant in 1975, another casualty of the Pastoral Measure of 1968. Despite the outstanding quality of its architecture and fittings, it did not pass into the care of the Redundant Churches Fund and in 1980 was designated for use for 'community purposes', highlighting the difficulties of finding suitable new uses for redundant churches.

CHRISTOPHER DALTON 1973

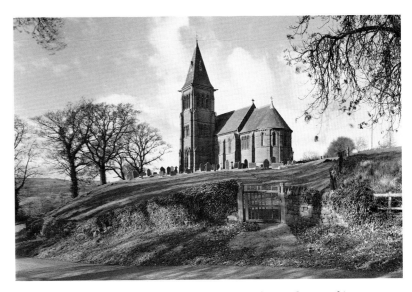

Ambassador's Staircase, Foreign Office, Westminster, London
Sir George Gilbert Scott's Foreign Office, designed in 1861 and completed in 1873, was the focus of a famous battle of the styles. Scott's enthusiasm for the Gothic was reflected in his first designs of 1856, but Parliament and Lord Palmerston rejected them in favour of the classical. Remarkably, Scott was able to alter completely his architectural style from the Gothic of St Pancras to produce the Italianate form of the Foreign Office. Photographed by the Royal Commission prior to an extensive restoration programme.

R.F. BRAYBROOK and A.M. RUMSEY, RCHME 1976

Church of the Holy Innocents, Highnam, Gloucestershire
The first major independent work by the architect Henry Woodyer, Holy Innocents (1849-51) is as remarkable for its sumptuous interior as for its architecture. Woodyer's client was Thomas Gambier Parry who himself executed the wall paintings in spirit fresco, a technique adapted from the Italian model and better suited to the English climate. Gordon Barnes' photographs of Victorian church architecture acquired in the course of the 1970s have proved to be an invaluable resource for a study of a once neglected and derided subject.

GORDON BARNES 1968

Hazelhurst, Endon and Stanley, Staffordshire
On the Caldon canal linking Leek with Stoke-on-Trent the isolated lock-keeper's cottage and the openwork cast-iron road bridge of 1842 form a characteristic industrial complex of earthworks, engineering structures and buildings which must be recorded as an ensemble if the context is to be understood.

1963 Staffordshire County Council

Windmill, Mill Hill, Peasenhall, Suffolk
The earliest form of windmill was the post mill in which the body of the mill was turned to face the sails to the wind. The 15th century saw the introduction of fixed towers with movable caps. The post mill on the left of this photograph was built in 1803. Its sails were shortened after one of them struck and killed a girl. In 1881 a smock mill from Cransford was re-erected at Peasenhall. The rebuilt stump appears on the right of the photograph. It no longer worked by wind power but was steam driven and continued to be used until the late 1970s. The post mill was dismantled in 1951.

H.E.S. SIMMONS 1935

John of Gaddesden's House, Little Gaddesden, Hertfordshire
Named as a result of a spurious connection with the late 14th-century Royal physician who
was a native of the village, this house of *c*1500 was probably intended for communal use,
perhaps as a marriage feast house or church hall. The quality and profusion of its ornament
is almost unparalleled in Hertfordshire vernacular architecture and is well demonstrated by this
carved corbel.

JOHN BASSHAM, RCHME 1977

The
1980s

The collections of the NBR have grown to the extent that the archive now contains more than one and a half million photographs. Among the more notable recent acquisitions have been the prints and negatives of factories and stationary engines taken over fifty years by George Watkins, the archive of photographs and prints of churches and cathedrals amassed by Gerald Cobb, the John Maltby collection of photographs of Odeon cinemas and Gordon Barnes's negatives of Victorian churches. Most important of all, at the end of the decade, has been the transfer to the NBR by the International Publishing Corporation of the huge store of negatives of country houses, their furnishings, decoration, gardens and estates, taken for Country Life from its foundation in 1897.

Appreciation of buildings of the very recent past has also developed in the 1980s. The demolition in 1980 of the 1928 Firestone factory, immediately prior to its formal protection, led to a rapid revision of the lists of historic buildings protected under the current legislation. The resurvey included many 20th-century buildings, but only those built before 1939. However, it was not long before the law was changed to allow the listing of buildings over thirty years old, and in exceptional circumstances even more recent structures.

The NBR has always included buildings of all dates – one of its most important collections being Herbert Felton's contemporary photographs of 1930s architecture acquired in 1947 – and now added to its archives are coverages of 1960s tower blocks, schools, churches and shopping centres. But historic architecture did not stop thirty years ago and in anticipation of the needs of the next half century, the National Buildings Record has photographed such modern masterpieces as Richard Rogers' building for Lloyds of London.

Monkton House, West Dean, West Sussex
Monkton was built in 1902 for William James to the designs of Edwin
Lutyens. The principal interest of the house lies in the alterations and
redecorations carried out for James's son Edward from the 1930s
onwards. Edward James was the foremost English supporter of
Surrealism and was particularly influenced by Salvador Dali. Monkton
was a unique example of the taste and decor of that period. Sadly, due
to lack of funds, the Trustees of the Edward James Foundation sold
the house in 1986. The Royal Commission's photographic coverage
was made shortly before the sale and dispersal of the contents.

Above Entrance Hall – showing the semi-circular staircase designed by
Christopher Nicholson.
Above right Principal Bathroom – lined with peach-coloured alabaster
and a backlit domed ceiling of green Styrian jade.

PETER WILLIAMS and PAT PAYNE, RCHME 1986

Right
De La Warr Pavilion, Bexhill, East Sussex
The construction of the De La Warr Pavilion was the result of a
controversial competition which was won by Erich Mendelsohn and
Serge Chermayeff. Earl De La Warr, Mayor of Bexhill from 1932-4 and
Chairman of the National Labour Party, sought to erect a socialist
pleasure palace by the sea. The Pavilion, which was completed in 1935,
represents in appearance and purpose a change from the traditional
seaside building, numbering among its attractions an auditorium
doubling as a cinema, a sun lounge and a reading room. The Pavilion
is currently undergoing major repair work to its exterior. Remedial
work to the original steel frame is needed to combat corrosion by the
sea air.

HERBERT FELTON 1937

Odeon Cinema, Burnley, Lancashire
Odeons had a distinctive house style which
was maintained by the use of standardised
designs for furnishings and fittings. This
reduced costs and increased the speed of
construction while establishing a consistent
image. Such totality of design, illustrated by
this 1937 example, rarely survives. John
Maltby was commissioned in the 1930s to
make a photographic record of the newly
completed cinemas and in 1985 the Royal
Commission purchased this invaluable
collection.

JOHN MALTBY 1937

Queen's Chapel, Marlborough Gate, Westminster, London
Separated from St James's Palace in 1809, this royal chapel is today only open to visitors during services so its importance as one of the few certain works by Inigo Jones to survive is little known. Built in 1627 and redecorated in 1680, this revolutionary classical style (the Venetian window is one of the first in England) helped to mould 18th-century taste.

DEREK KENDALL, RCHME 1988

Wall Painting, Rochester Cathedral, Kent
On the north choir wall of Rochester Cathedral is a mid 13th-century realisation of a subject common to both medieval art and literature: The Wheel of Fortune. The mutability of human fortunes is symbolised by the depiction of a man trapped within the spokes of a wheel which is turned by a female representation of Fate. At the top of the wheel an enthroned king is about to fall from his perch. The principal figures are painted in rich tones of red and orange on a green background diapered with roses. It is thought to be contemporary with two Wheels of Fortune which Henry III had painted at the palaces of Winchester (1235) and Clarendon (1247).

LEN FURBANK, RCHME 1982

Malmesbury, Wiltshire
The high viewpoint and the careful composition by a local photographer provide in one image much useful information not only about the state of the Abbey ruin and the market cross but also about the domestic building materials and the density of the medieval town.

W. HANKS 1864

Left
Kedleston Hall, Derbyshire
The marble hall completed in the 1780s was described by Pevsner as 'one of the most magnificent apartments of the 18th century in England'. Kedleston has a complicated building history but the principal contributor was the architect Robert Adam who took charge in 1760 of works already in progress. The house has recently been acquired by the National Trust with assistance from the National Heritage Memorial Fund after a period of uncertainty as to its future.

PETER WILLIAMS, RCHME 1987

Whitacre Pumping Station, Shustoke, Warwickshire

The waterworks was designed c1860 for Birmingham Corporation by local architects Martin and Chamberlain. These extremely impressive and elaborate beam engines were built in 1884 by James Watt & Co. They ran until 1936, when they were superseded by more modern turbines, but remained on standby until 1948 when one was scrapped and the other moved to Birmingham Science Museum. The photographer George Watkins made a lifetime study of stationary engines and his collection came to the NBR at his death in 1989.

GEORGE WATKINS 1936

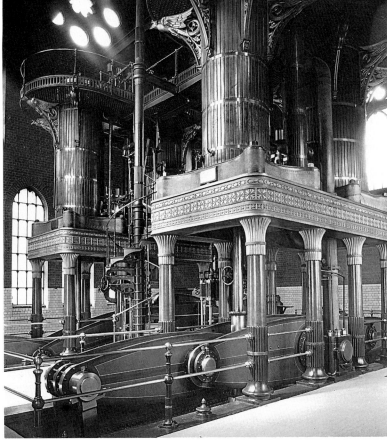

Williton Hospital, Williton, Somerset

Changes in the nature of health care during the 1980s has resulted in many hospital buildings becoming redundant. This has prompted the Royal Commission to commence a national survey of historic hospitals. George Gilbert Scott and William Moffat designed Williton as a workhouse in 1837; it was later converted to a hospital, but its future is now in doubt.

PAT PAYNE, RCHME 1989

Fylingdales, North Yorkshire
These early warning radar aerials built in
1962 constitute monuments of a high
sculptural and engineering order, set in a
featureless landscape which emphasizes their
bizarre simplicity and huge scale. Such
modern military and industrial structures
must be selectively recorded when they
become redundant so that the archive holds
representative records of contemporary as
well as historical sites.

TONY PERRY, RCHME 1988

East Lighthouse, Sutton Bridge, Lincolnshire
As part of improvements on the River Nene
two lighthouses were built at the mouth in
1826-30. This photograph shows the east
bank lighthouse which was the home of the
naturalist Peter Scott, 1933-9. It was while
living here that he developed his idea of the
Wild Fowl Trust. Since the Royal Commission
made its photographic coverage the tower has
been incorporated as part of a modern house.

PETER WILLIAMS, RCHME 1981

Walton Colliery, Walton, West Yorkshire
Walton Colliery was a branch of the New Sharlton Colliery Company. The first shaft was sunk in 1890 and the colliery reached the peak of its production in the early 20th century. It is unusual in having remained little altered since that time. This photograph shows Number 1 Shaft (right), of typical late 19th-century lattice ironwork construction, and Number 2 Shaft, built in 1923, which became the main shaft for bringing up coal. The rapid changes in the coal industry present a new challenge in recording industrial complexes.

TERRY BUCHANAN, RCHME 1981

Odeon Cinema, Peckham, Southwark, London
Art Deco styling was a hallmark of early Odeon designs commissioned by Oscar Deutsch in the 1930s. This example is seen here at night with its distinctive neon lighting and the familiar squared lettering of the name. Peckham Odeon was designed by Andrew Mather and opened in June 1938. It was demolished in 1985.

JOHN MALTBY 1938

The 1980s

Hatfield, Hertfordshire

George Frampton's seated figure of the
Marquess of Salisbury (1830-1903), at
Hatfield House, was erected in 1906 to
commemorate the owner of the house who
held office as Prime Minister three times. Paul
Barkshire has devoted his career to
photographing historic buildings on large-
format negatives of exceptional quality.

PAUL BARKSHIRE 1984

**Ascent to the Hanging Wood, Iford Manor,
Iford, Wiltshire**

In 1895 the architect H.A. Peto retired to Italy
owing to ill health. He devoted himself to the
study and design of Italian gardens and
established a considerable reputation in this
field. The acquisition of Iford in 1899
afforded him the opportunity to create his
own Italianate landscape, furnished with
statuary and antiquities collected on the
continent. The 1980s has been the decade of
garden history as a serious study and the
Country Life Collection, which includes
photographs of Iford in 1907 and 1922, is an
invaluable resource.

1922, © Country Life

Lloyd's Building, Leadenhall Street, City of London
The chorus of opinions and tastes expressed in response to such a controversial structure as Richard Rogers' Lloyd's Building made it quite clear even before it was finished in 1986, that it was worth recording. Many less well-known post-war buildings, now at risk through obsolescence, are being monitored for selective recording.

PETER WILLIAMS, RCHME 1990

**Trellick Tower, Golborne Road, Kensington
and Chelsea, London**
One of the most distinctive tower blocks in
London, the Trellick Tower was designed in
1967 by Erno Goldfinger who, unlike most
contemporary architects, actually lived in his
own creation. The NBR in conjunction with
the Courtauld Institute of Art has undertaken
a survey of the more important and influential
post-war buildings to ensure that the
collection is kept up to date.

PHILIP WARD-JACKSON 1989,
© *Courtauld Institute of Art*

Albert Dock, Liverpool, Merseyside
At the time when it was photographed the
future of this robust and elegant complex,
which now incorporates the Tate Gallery of
the North, was by no means assured. Built by
Jesse Hartley in 1845, docks such as this
became redundant in many ports and a
national programme of recording became
vital well before the conservation of surviving
examples.

PETER WILLIAMS, RCHME 1981

Church of St Nicholas, Stanford on Avon, Northamptonshire
St Peter, from an almost complete set of figures of Apostles, stands in the north-east chancel window. The choir glazing can be dated on heraldic evidence to c1315-16 and contributes to what is one of the most extensive parish church glazing schemes of the early 14th century. Photographic recording is now carried out by the RCHME in all of the principal stained glass conservation studios. This panel was photographed at Barley Studios near York.

BOB SKINGLE, RCHME 1987

INDEX